MY
RAMADAN
COLORING BOOK
with good deeds checklist

_____

_____

_____

RAMADAN

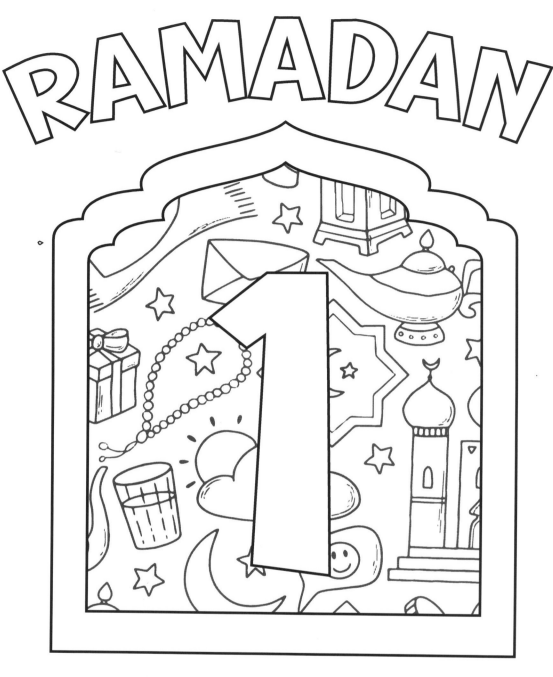

MY GOOD DEEDS CHECKLIST

I prayed ☐

I did a mini fast ☐

I made dua ☐

I read Quran ☐

I helped someone ☐

I gave charity ☐

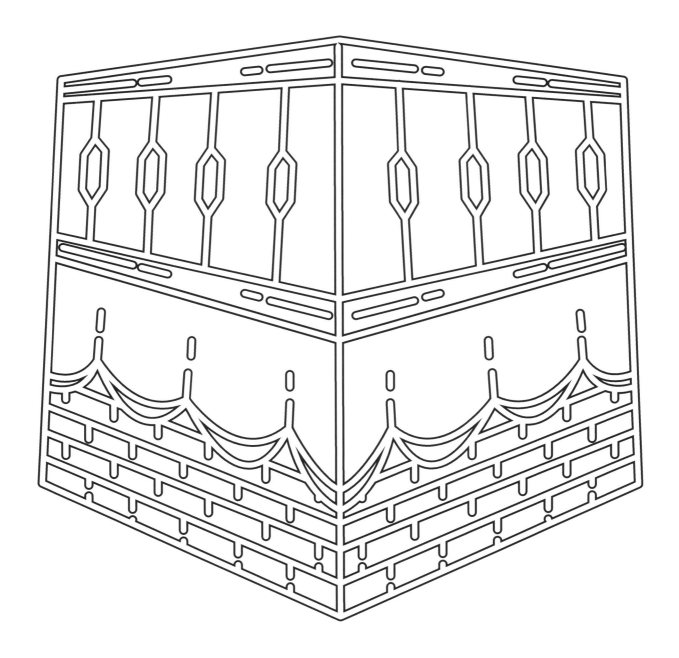

RAMADAN KAREEM

RAMADAN

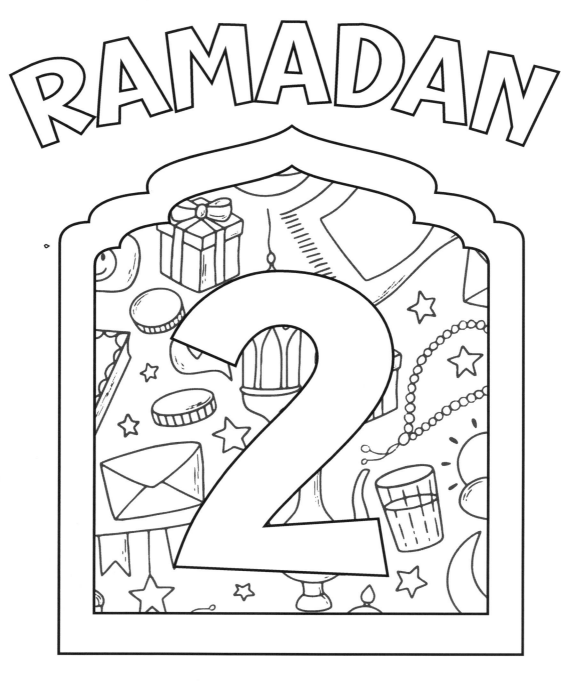

MY GOOD DEEDS CHECKLIST

I prayed ☐

I did a mini fast ☐

I made dua ☐

I read Quran ☐

I helped someone ☐

I gave charity ☐

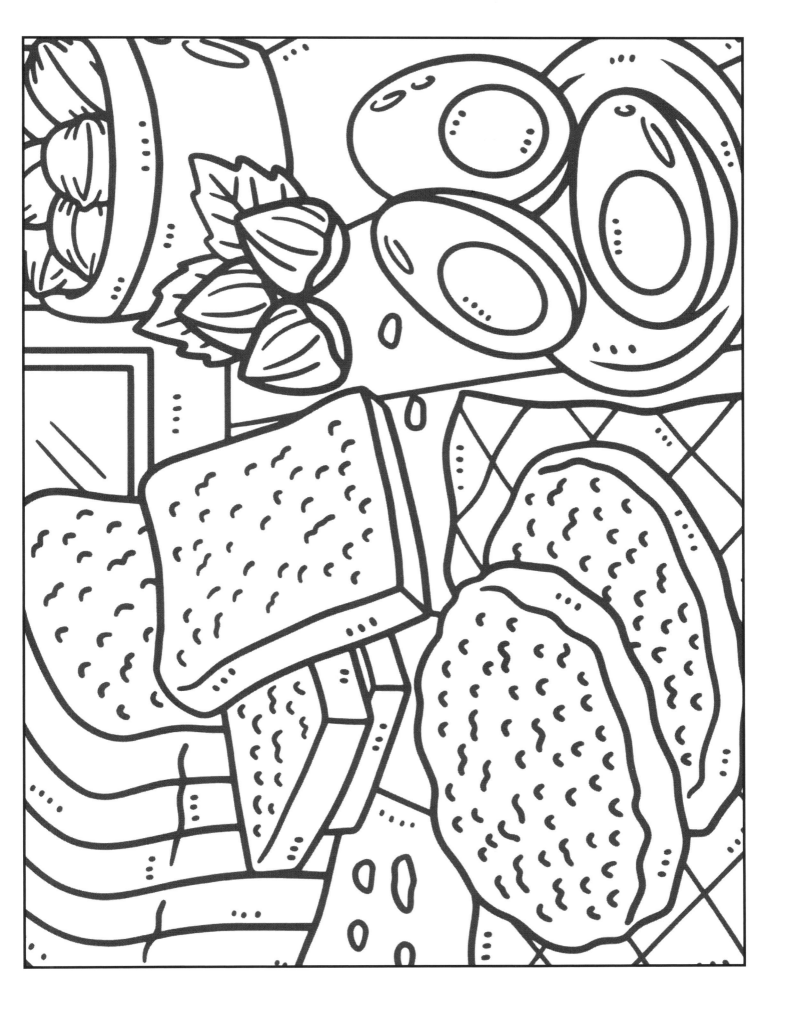

RAMADAN

MY GOOD DEEDS CHECKLIST

I prayed ☐

I did a mini fast ☐

I made dua ☐

I read Quran ☐

I helped someone ☐

I gave charity ☐

RAMADAN

MY GOOD DEEDS CHECKLIST

I prayed ☐

I did a mini fast ☐

I made dua ☐

I read Quran ☐

I helped someone ☐

I gave charity ☐

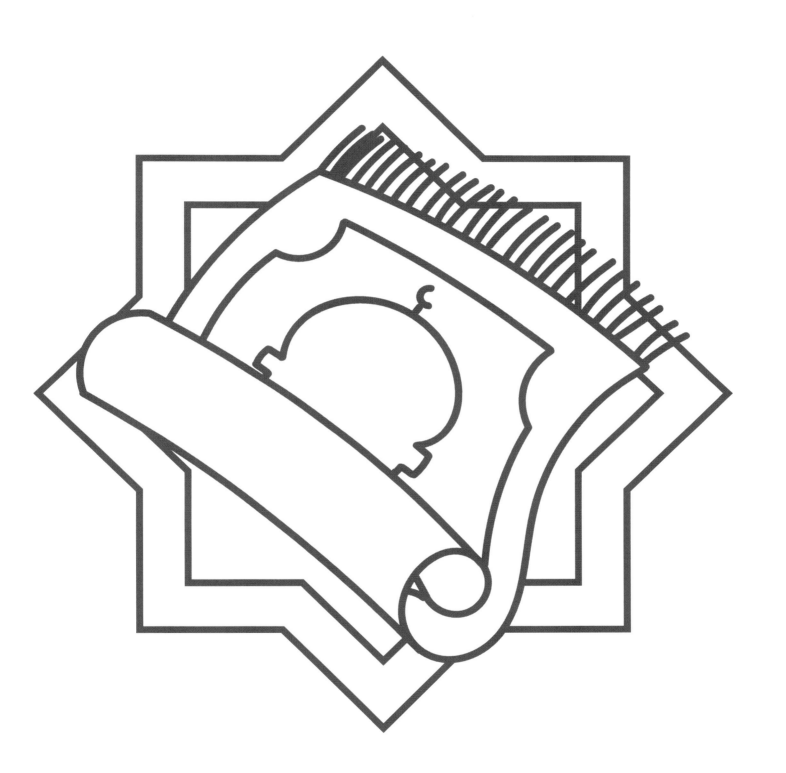

RAMADAN

MY GOOD DEEDS CHECKLIST

I prayed ☐

I did a mini fast ☐

I made dua ☐

I read Quran ☐

I helped someone ☐

I gave charity ☐

RAMADAN

MY GOOD DEEDS CHECKLIST

I prayed ☐

I did a mini fast ☐

I made dua ☐

I read Quran ☐

I helped someone ☐

I gave charity ☐

RAMADAN

MY GOOD DEEDS CHECKLIST

I prayed ☐

I did a mini fast ☐

I made dua ☐

I read Quran ☐

I helped someone ☐

I gave charity ☐

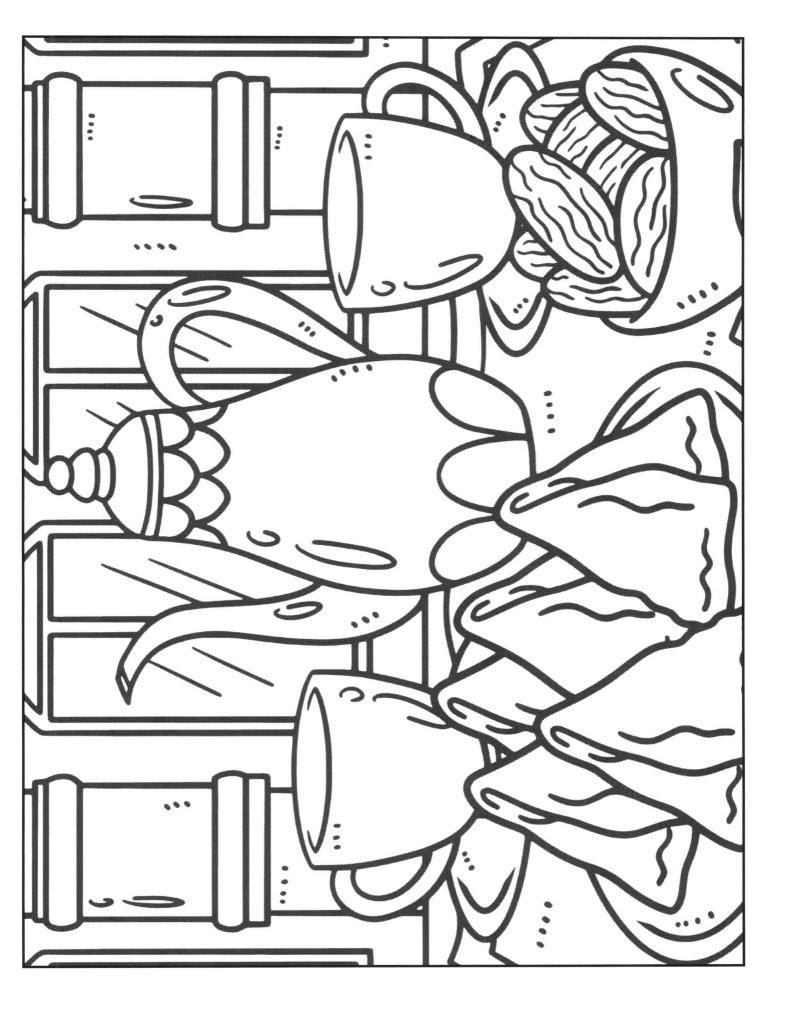

RAMADAN

MY GOOD DEEDS CHECKLIST

I prayed ☐

I did a mini fast ☐

I made dua ☐

I read Quran ☐

I helped someone ☐

I gave charity ☐

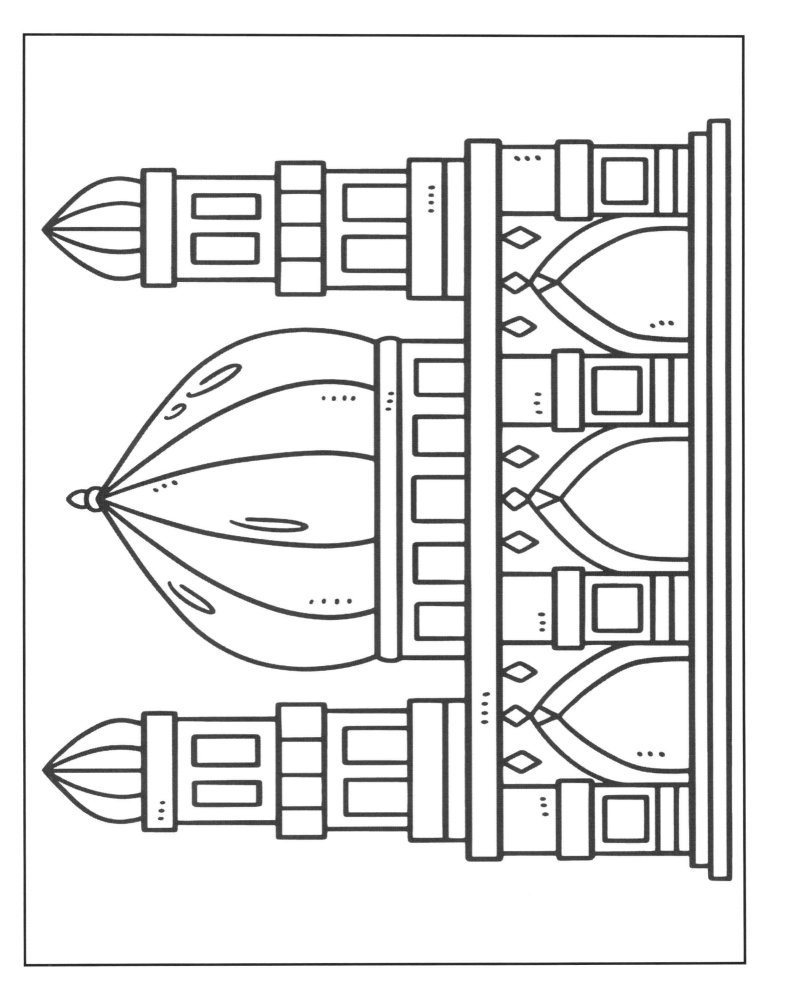

RAMADAN

MY GOOD DEEDS CHECKLIST

I prayed ☐

I did a mini fast ☐

I made dua ☐

I read Quran ☐

I helped someone ☐

I gave charity ☐

RAMADAN

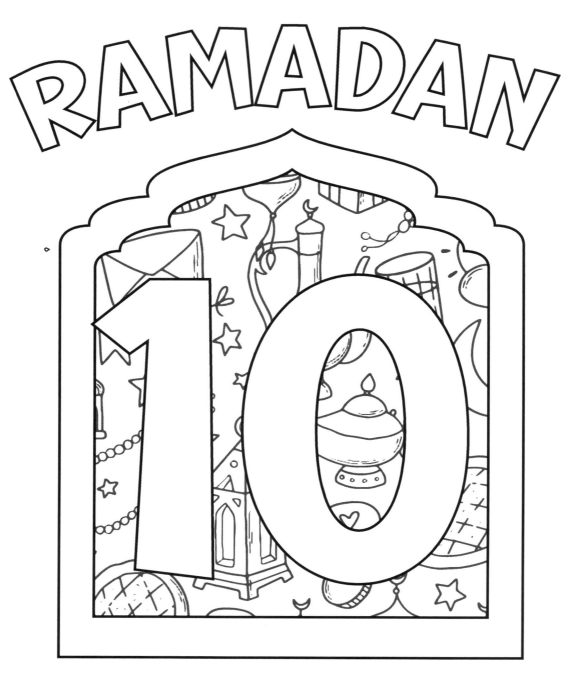

MY GOOD DEEDS CHECKLIST

I prayed ☐

I did a mini fast ☐

I made dua ☐

I read Quran ☐

I helped someone ☐

I gave charity ☐

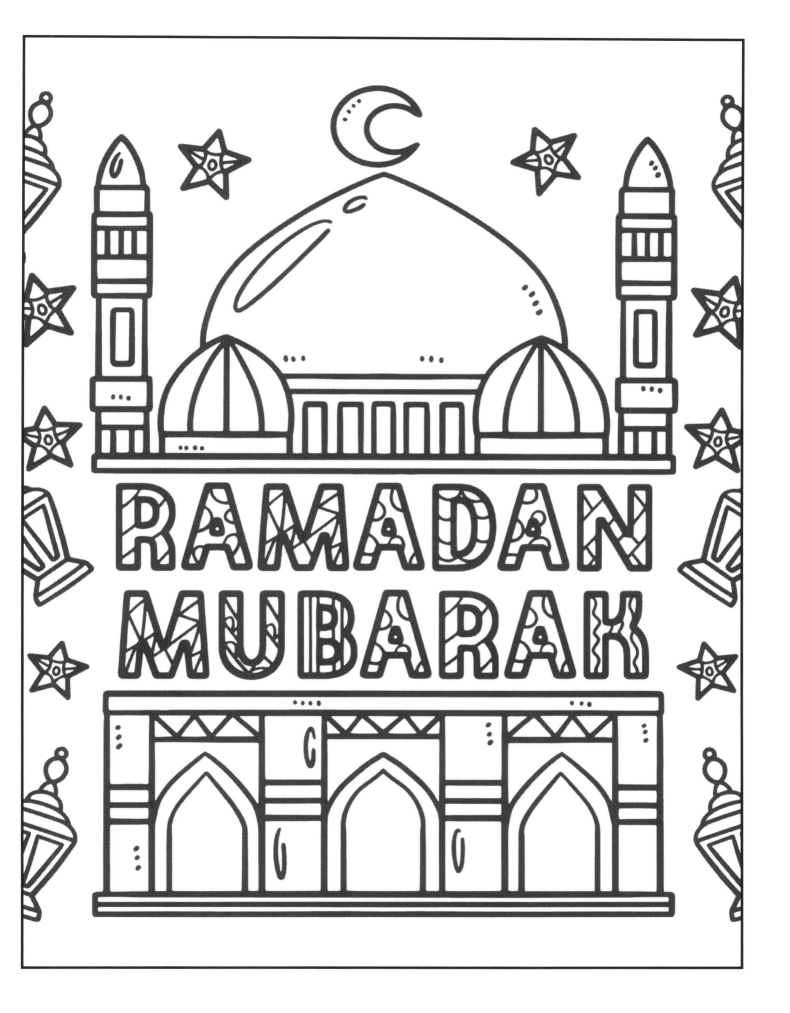

RAMADAN

MY GOOD DEEDS CHECKLIST

I prayed ☐

I did a mini fast ☐

I made dua ☐

I read Quran ☐

I helped someone ☐

I gave charity ☐

RAMADAN

MY GOOD DEEDS CHECKLIST

I prayed ☐

I did a mini fast ☐

I made dua ☐

I read Quran ☐

I helped someone ☐

I gave charity ☐

RAMADAN

MY GOOD DEEDS CHECKLIST

I prayed ☐

I did a mini fast ☐

I made dua ☐

I read Quran ☐

I helped someone ☐

I gave charity ☐

RAMADAN

MY GOOD DEEDS CHECKLIST

I prayed ☐

I did a mini fast ☐

I made dua ☐

I read Quran ☐

I helped someone ☐

I gave charity ☐

RAMADAN

MY GOOD DEEDS CHECKLIST

I prayed ☐

I did a mini fast ☐

I made dua ☐

I read Quran ☐

I helped someone ☐

I gave charity ☐

RAMADAN

MY GOOD DEEDS CHECKLIST

I prayed ☐

I did a mini fast ☐

I made dua ☐

I read Quran ☐

I helped someone ☐

I gave charity ☐

RAMADAN

MY GOOD DEEDS CHECKLIST

I prayed	☐
I did a mini fast	☐
I made dua	☐
I read Quran	☐
I helped someone	☐
I gave charity	☐

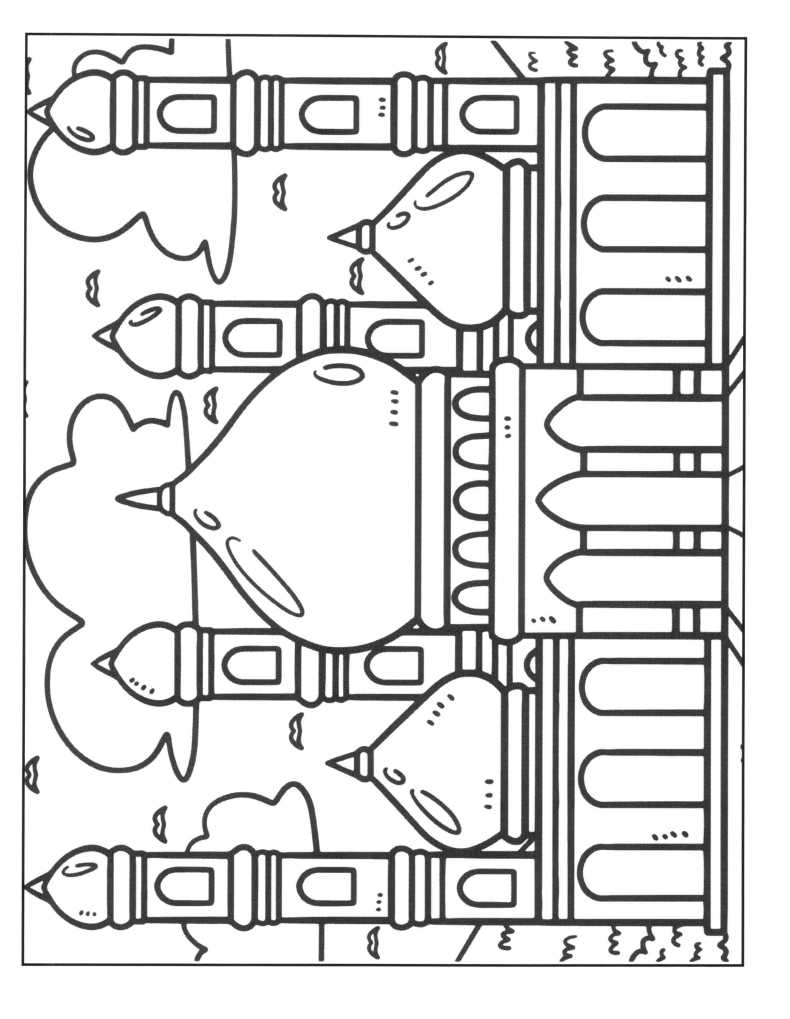

RAMADAN

MY GOOD DEEDS CHECKLIST

I prayed ☐

I did a mini fast ☐

I made dua ☐

I read Quran ☐

I helped someone ☐

I gave charity ☐

RAMADAN

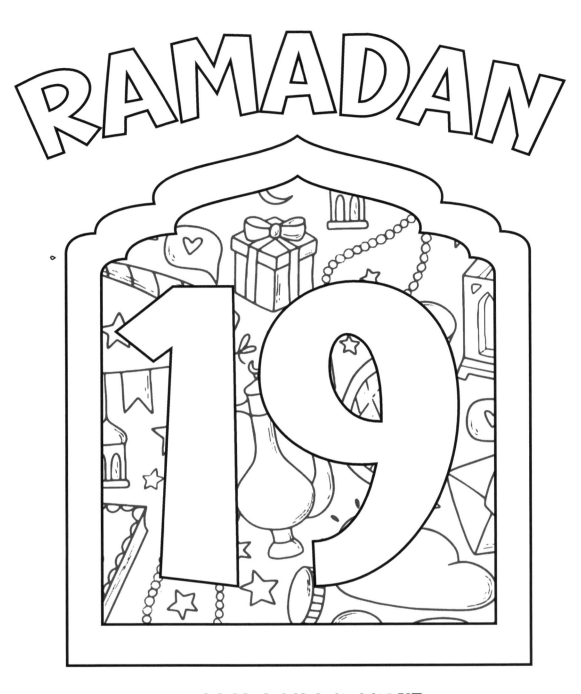

MY GOOD DEEDS CHECKLIST

I prayed ☐

I did a mini fast ☐

I made dua ☐

I read Quran ☐

I helped someone ☐

I gave charity ☐

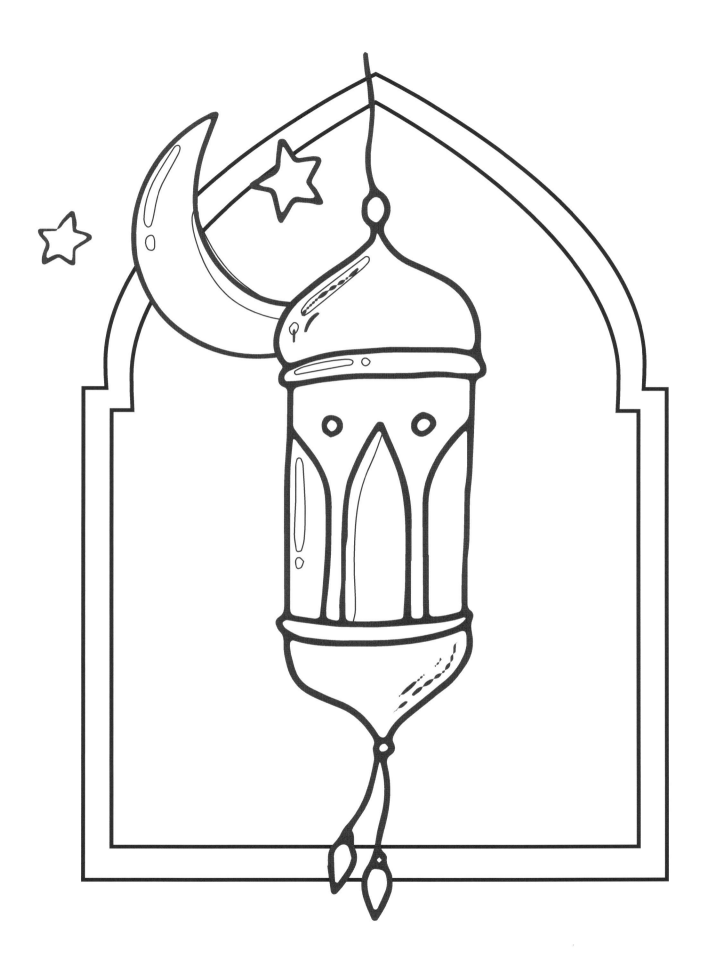

RAMADAN

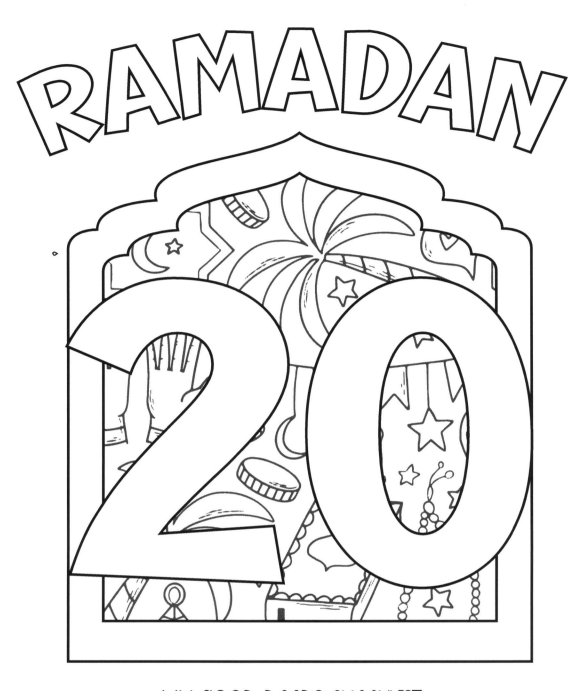

MY GOOD DEEDS CHECKLIST

I prayed ☐

I did a mini fast ☐

I made dua ☐

I read Quran ☐

I helped someone ☐

I gave charity ☐

RAMADAN MUBARAK

RAMADAN

MY GOOD DEEDS CHECKLIST

I prayed ☐

I did a mini fast ☐

I made dua ☐

I read Quran ☐

I helped someone ☐

I gave charity ☐

RAMADAN

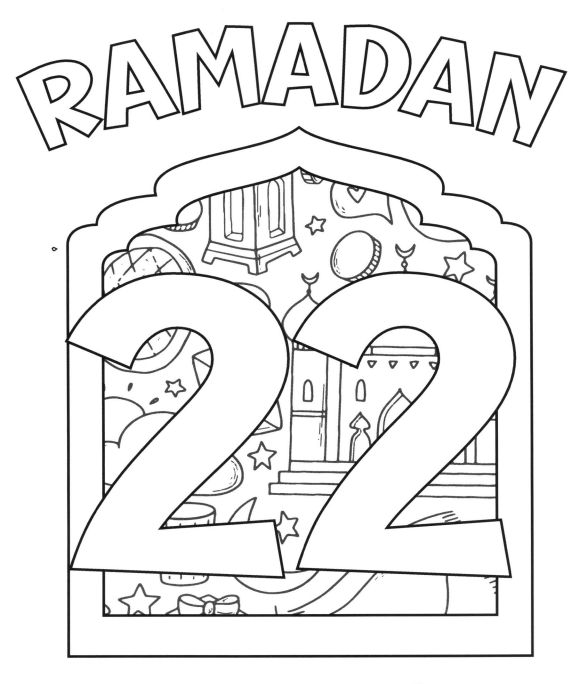

MY GOOD DEEDS CHECKLIST

I prayed ☐

I did a mini fast ☐

I made dua ☐

I read Quran ☐

I helped someone ☐

I gave charity ☐

RAMADAN

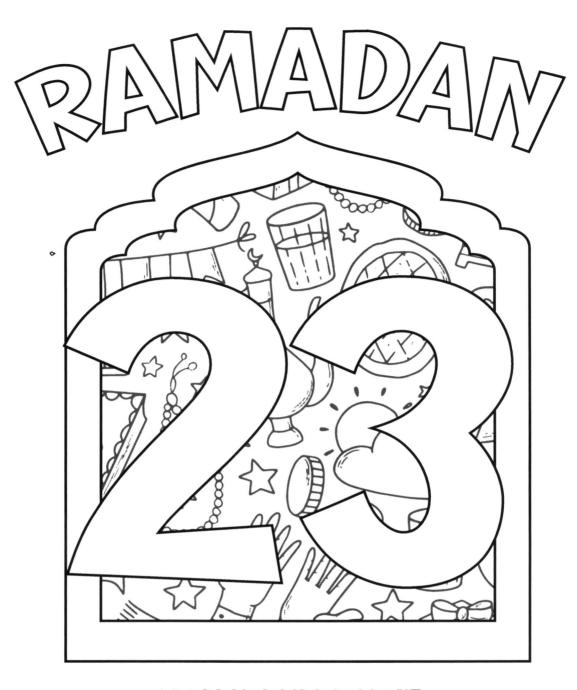

MY GOOD DEEDS CHECKLIST

I prayed ☐

I did a mini fast ☐

I made dua ☐

I read Quran ☐

I helped someone ☐

I gave charity ☐

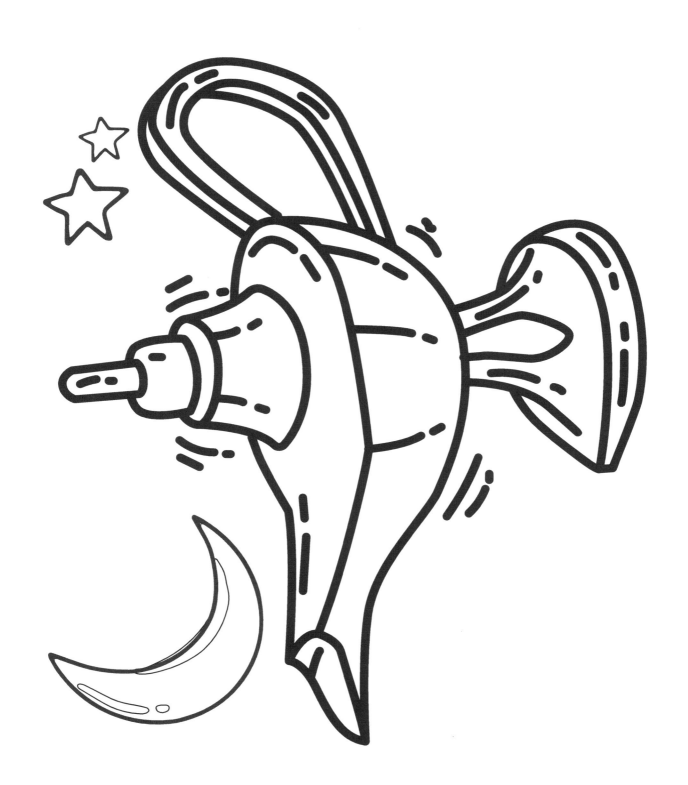

RAMADAN

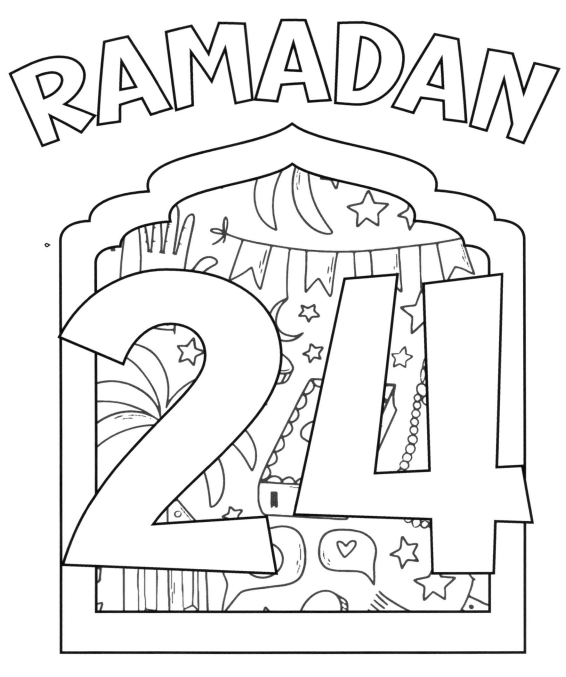

MY GOOD DEEDS CHECKLIST

I prayed ☐

I did a mini fast ☐

I made dua ☐

I read Quran ☐

I helped someone ☐

I gave charity ☐

RAMADAN

MY GOOD DEEDS CHECKLIST

I prayed ☐

I did a mini fast ☐

I made dua ☐

I read Quran ☐

I helped someone ☐

I gave charity ☐

RAMADAN

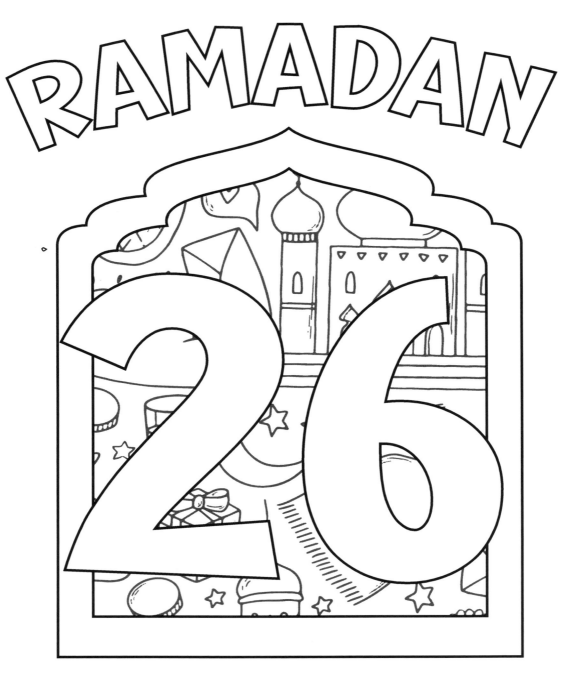

MY GOOD DEEDS CHECKLIST

I prayed ☐

I did a mini fast ☐

I made dua ☐

I read Quran ☐

I helped someone ☐

I gave charity ☐

RAMADAN

MY GOOD DEEDS CHECKLIST

I prayed ☐

I did a mini fast ☐

I made dua ☐

I read Quran ☐

I helped someone ☐

I gave charity ☐

RAMADAN

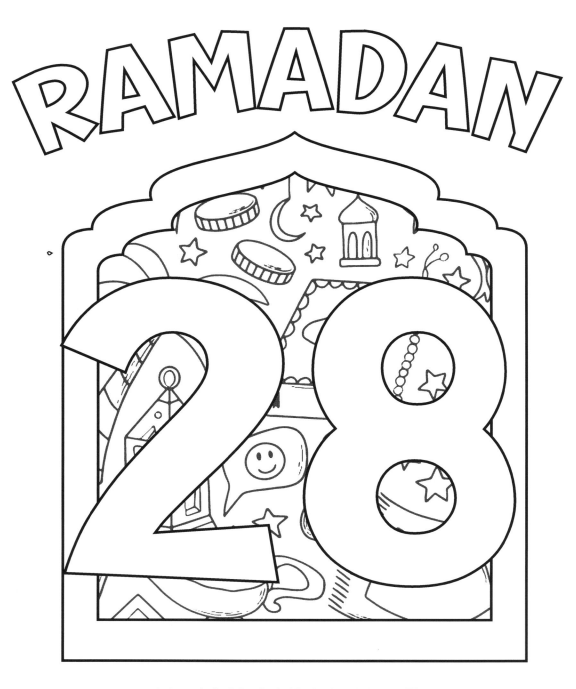

MY GOOD DEEDS CHECKLIST

I prayed ☐

I did a mini fast ☐

I made dua ☐

I read Quran ☐

I helped someone ☐

I gave charity ☐

RAMADAN

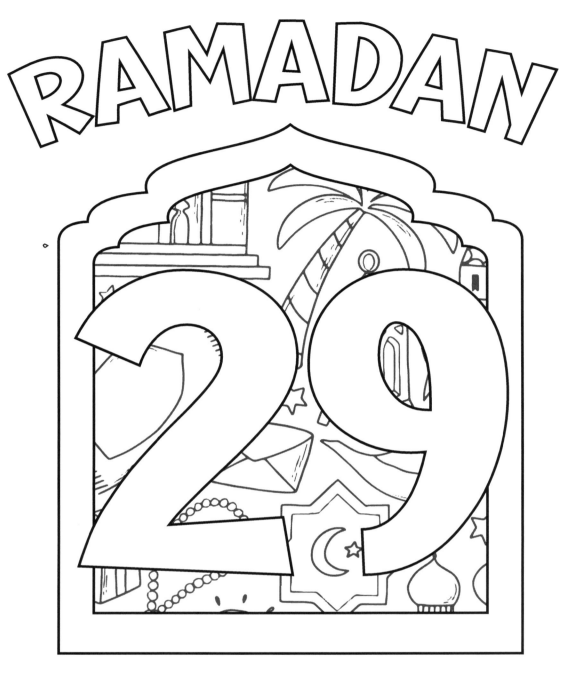

MY GOOD DEEDS CHECKLIST

I prayed ☐

I did a mini fast ☐

I made dua ☐

I read Quran ☐

I helped someone ☐

I gave charity ☐

RAMADAN

MY GOOD DEEDS CHECKLIST

I prayed ☐

I did a mini fast ☐

I made dua ☐

I read Quran ☐

I helped someone ☐

I gave charity ☐

Made in United States
Troutdale, OR
03/04/2024